Dark Unicorn

Written by Danny Pearson

Illustrated by Christian Cornia

Collins

1 Loud music

Blue the unicorn liked music.

One day, she met a band.

"I'm Spark. Play with us," said the harp player.

"Cool. I enjoy rock music," Blue replied.

Spark started playing. It sounded soft and soothing.

But Blue found it annoying.

"I like loud music," said Blue.

Spark was annoyed and said "Loud music is stupid!" Blue felt sad.

Blue felt like the odd one out.
So, she ran.

She didn't stop until she reached the wood.

2 The wood

It was dark and damp in the wood.
Blue shivered.

Then there was music. It was loud music.

"What a sound!" Blue cried.
She spied a form in the gloom.

In a swirl of mist, a beast appeared.
"Play music with us," the beast said.

Blue met the beast's band.

Fox was the lead singer.

Blue tried playing with the band.
At first it was hard.
"I'll lead," said Fox. "You join in!"

Blue started playing to the beat.
"You sound terrific!" cried Fox.

"Now we are a real band," said the beast.
"We are Dark Unicorn!" cried Fox.
"Let's play a gig."

3 The gig

The sports ground was full.

The gig was about to start.

"How shall we play?" said Blue.

"Play loud!" replied the beast.

The crowd were singing.

"You rock, Blue!" cried the beast. "Jump in!"

"I feel so cool!" Blue cried.
Blue was loud and proud!

Map

🐾 Review: After reading 🐾

Use your assessment from hearing the children read to choose any GPCs, words or tricky words that need additional practice.

Read 1: Decoding

- Discuss the following words that have more than one meaning, encouraging the children to explain the correct meaning by referring to the context.
  - page 3: **Cool** (*an expression meaning "great"; Blue likes the music, and wouldn't be talking about the weather*)
  - page 3: **rock** (*a type of loud music; it's paired with "music" so describes the type of music*)
- Turn to page 2 and ask the children to find two words containing the /yoo/ sound. (*music, unicorn*)
  - Ask the children to find a word containing the /oo/ sound. (*Blue*) Ask: Which letters make the sound? (*ue*)
- Challenge the children to pick a favourite page and read each word by blending the sounds in their head, silently, before reading the whole page aloud.

Read 2: Prosody

- Reread pages 4–7, asking children to think about how the characters are feeling.
- Let children take it in turns to read Blue's words on page 6 with an enthusiastic tone.
- Then let them take it in turns to read Spark's words on page 7 in a cross, loud tone.
- Turn to page 12 and challenge the children to read Blue's spoken words. Ask: How is Blue feeling now?

Read 3: Comprehension

- Discuss the kind of music children enjoy listening to and playing. Ask: How does it make you feel?
- Compare the bands on pages 3 and 17.
  - Which band does Blue like best? (*Dark Unicorn on page 21*)
  - Discuss with the children: How are the bands different?
  - Talk about preferences and how one person might like soothing music and another, loud music.
- Focus on the pair of opposites: soothing / annoying.
  - Discuss the meanings of **soothing** and **annoying**. Can the children think of other sounds that are soothing or annoying. (e.g. *soothing sea, birdsong; annoying traffic, washing machine sounds*)
  - Challenge the children to think of a synonym for each word, or to look through other books for similar words. (e.g. *relaxing, calming; irritating, disturbing*)
- Look together at pages 22 and 23. Ask the children to use the pictures to help them retell the story in their own words.